Painting Landscapes

IN WATERCOLORS

Author: Parramón Ediciones Editorial Team
Illustrator: Vicenç Ballestar

All inquiries should be addressed to:
Barron's Educational Series, Inc.
250 Wireless Boulevard
Hauppauge, New York 11788

Library of Congress Catalog Card No. 95-37534

International Standard Book No. 0-8120-9399-2

Library of Congress Cataloging-in-Publication Data
Paisajes a la acuarela. English.
  Painting landscapes in watercolors / [author, Parramón
Ediciones Editorial Team ; illustrator, Vicenç Ballestar].
    p.   cm. — (Easy painting and drawing)
  ISBN 0-8120-9399-2
  1. Watercolor painting—Technique.   2. Landscape
painting—Technique.   I. Ballestar, Vicenç.   II. Parramón
Ediciones Editorial Team.   III. Title.   IV. Series.
ND2240.P3513   1996
751.42'2436—dc20   95-37534
                                                      CIP

Printed in Spain
6789   9960   987654321

IN WATERCOLORS

Painting Landscapes

BARRON'S

CONTENTS

Introduction **5**

Watercolor Materials **6**

Watercolor Techniques **10**

Exercises

Painting a Mountain Landscape **16**

Painting a Cloudy Landscape **22**

Painting Trees and a River **30**

Painting a Track through a Snow-covered
   Forest **36**

Painting a Composition Centered on
   a Tree **44**

Painting Snow-covered Peaks at Dusk **50**

Painting a Landscape from an Elevated
   Point of View **58**

Acknowledgments **64**

L andscapes have always been an appealing and rewarding theme for the sensitive artist. A landscape is always unique: The light that illuminates it changes; it may contain clouds; sunlight may bathe it profusely; its outlines may be shrouded in mist or fog, or masked by rain, or covered by a blanket of snow. The colors and elements also vary: In winter, the trees are bare, and gray tones predominate; in spring, the colors are green, and in summer, the tones are warmer. The fall brings a great variety of colors and tones (reds, browns, oranges, yellows). Even during a single day, the light changes constantly, from dawn to dusk. It is practically impossible to find any other subject matter that undergoes as many changes in appearance as a landscape. We have mentioned only a few transformations, but if you are observant enough, you will find a whole host of tonalities and different hues related to the planes and atmosphere in which the elements are situated.

Since you will not always carry your brushes and easel when you are out for a stroll in the country, make sure you always have a sketch pad and a soft pencil handy to draw notes and record details that may be useful when painting. Sketching the theme will enable you to find the appropriate composition, searching out varying points of view. Drawing notes of a single landscape on different days will enable you to notice a landscape's numerous aspects. This is a good exercise in interpretation and synthesis that will teach you to observe a landscape in many ways. The fact that you are going to paint in watercolors is yet another reason to take notes. Watercolor is an appealing, exciting technique because of its freshness, looseness, and spontaneity. However, before embarking on any picture, you should have it well planned. A sketch or color note is the one essential aid that enables you to see what your painting will be like before you start.

The exercises contained in this book will provide you with ample practice in this genre. However, do not forget that the most important factors for achieving a good painting are your imagination and creativity—that is, your personality.

We wish you the best of luck in your endeavor and hope you will find it gratifying.

Jordi Vigué

WATERCOLOR MATERIALS

Water is an indispensable element of watercolor painting. More over, water determines the type of paper and brushes used, as well as the characteristic method of painting with them. A medium textured sheet of paper, a soft brush, a few colors, and water are all you require to get going. Specially manufactured watercolor paper is available in stores. The brushes come in a wide range of types and sizes. The same goes for the colors. It is a question of knowing what you want. Let us now look at the characteristics of these materials.

PAPER

There are several different thicknesses and textures of watercolor paper. They tend to be distinguished by weight (measured in pounds). Medium-textured, or cold-pressed, paper is the most common type used, especially in a painting under 20 inches in length. The quality and brand of the paper can be identified by the watermark, which can be seen by holding the sheet up to light. Watercolor paper is sold in individual sheets, in blocks attached to a backing, or in pads. Since pads are sturdy, there is no need to paint with a drawing board; the sheets in a watercolor block are "bound" with plastic glue on all four sides, and you must remove each sheet with a knife when you have finished painting.

BRUSHES

Your local art store should stock a wide variety of sizes and shapes of brushes. The best quality brushes are made of sable. They are soft and hold plenty of water. Furthermore, they maintain their pointed tips much longer than other brushes do and are therefore the most expensive. Cheaper quality brushes are made of ox hair and mongoose hair. Synthetic fiber is an economic option that provides good results in flat brushes.

| CADMIUM YELLOW PALE | CADMIUM ORANGE | YELLOW OCHRE | BURNT SIENNA | VAN DYCK BROWN | CADMIUM RED LIGHT | CARMINE |

COLORS AND ACCESSORIES

At the bottom of these pages you can see a selection of recommended colors. There is an almost infinite number of colors available, but no watercolor artist uses them all. Dry colors come in pans that can be purchased individually or in palette-box sets. Watercolors are also available in tubes that must be placed on a plastic or metal palette. You will also need large water containers with wide mouths; adhesive tape, for attaching the paper to a drawing board; soft lead pencils; charcoal; a rubber eraser; a knife; and a natural sponge for dampening large areas. In addition, it is also advisable to have a roll of absorbent paper handy for dabbing or removing excess water.

| YELLOWISH GREEN | OLIVE GREEN | SAP GREEN | COBALT BLUE | ULTRAMARINE BLUE | CERULEAN BLUE | INDIGO |

STRETCHING THE PAPER

You can stretch a sheet of paper with adhesive tape. This will prevent the paper from forming ripples or puckers when it is dampened by the watercolors. You can also use a stretcher, treating the paper as if it were a canvas. The accompanying photographs show the process. First, dampen the paper with a sponge and abundant water (A); then, place the stretcher over the paper, leaving a sufficient margin of 3 or 4 inches around the edges (B); next, fold each side over the frame of the stretcher (C); and finally fold the corners over as if you were wrapping up the stretcher and attach them with drawing pins (D). Once it is dry, the paper should be perfectly stretched without any ripples or puckers (E). Place some wrapping paper over the back of the stretched paper to protect it, and stick it in place with adhesive tape (F).

A

B

C

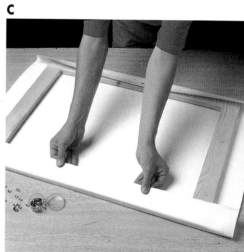

D

E

F

STRETCHING

Since a fine-quality watercolor paper in 300-pound weight is extremely heavy, it does not need to be stretched and can be worked on without previous preparation. However, this type of paper may warp when you are working with abundant water. For this reason some artists stretch their paper so that it reverts to its original smoothness once it dries. It must be noted, though, that the paper's original shape is recovered when it is framed, no matter how many times it has been painted over.

ACCESSORIES FOR PAINTING OUTDOORS

Landscapes must be painted from nature. To work outdoors, you will need a few extra accessories. First, it is essential to have a portable easel. The metallic ones are very light and sturdy, and are easy to carry and to set up. The easel par excellence, however, is the French-style easel, with a tray for the palette and a compartment for the brushes and colors. Other important accessories include a folder for carrying the paper (with drawing pins for attaching them), a wooden drawing board, a sketch pad, a bottle of water, a folding stool, and a hat during the summer when the sun is high.

COLOR LOSES ITS INTENSITY

It is important to remember that watercolors lose between 10 and 20 percent of their intensity once they have dried. This loss is especially evident when the picture is painted outdoors, in the sun. It is essential to anticipate this and intensify the tones you want be strongest, recognizing that they will fade slightly after they have dried.

TECHNIQUES

Watercolor has its own special techniques that painters must employ if they are to paint successful pictures. This is to say that it is essential to exploit the possibilities of the use of water in the treatment of color, the way the brush is employed to create forms, and the techniques available to create the different effects that can be achieved only with this medium. Let us examine them.

OPENING UP WHITES

You can lift out, or "open up," an area over a previously painted area that has dried. This is done by rubbing the surface with a clean brush soaked in water and so dissolving the dry color. Then use a dry brush to absorb the water, thus opening up the white. This technique is very useful for making corrections or for lightening color, to paint a cloud, for instance.

In the adjacent photographs you can see the process: by dampening an area and then absorbing the moisture, you can open up a white area in a desired shape (thanks to the way in which the paper is rubbed with the brush). Details can be added to this type of cloud with different hues of the color used to give it volume and bring out the shape.

LIGHTENING AND DARKENING

Using the previously explained technique, we can also create a series of light and dark gradations that can be used to depict mountains and clouds on the horizon of the landscape. In this situation we gradually lift out color in strips going from dark to light. We will start on the darker areas, using little water, and continue with the lighter ones, gradually adding more water and also absorbing it to remove the background color.

Gradual darkening is obtained by applying successive thin layers over each other in increasingly greater concentrations, always allowing one layer to dry before painting the next. The result of these two actions is the intensification of the planes or zones of color by working with one single tone.

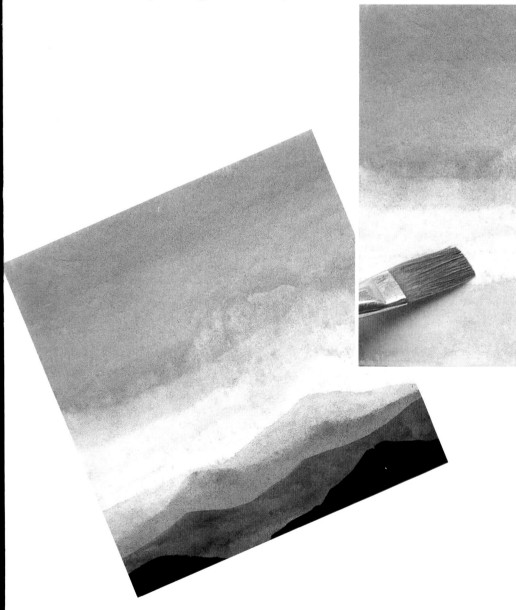

THE USE OF ABSORBENT PAPER

Absorbent paper is very useful for lifting or lightening color. As we mentioned before, to open up a white area, you first have to dampen the surface of the dry color and then absorb the water containing the dissolved paint with a dry brush. You can do the same with absorbent paper; in fact, the operation is more effective, since you can completely dry the sheet and repeat the process if necessary.

COMPOSING A LANDSCAPE

To compose is to arrange the subject matter you have before you on the paper. We cannot take in the entire landscape only a part of it, and even then we have to organize it in the most attractive way. This organization is almost always present in nature itself—the painter has only to perceive it and know how to represent it by emphasizing the significant aspects and leaving out what confuses. These images are just a few examples of what composition is all about. Next to each one of these watercolors we have reproduced preliminary sketches in which you can make out the essential lines and masses. Before you paint the theme you have chosen, you should draw a couple of these sketches to determine the landscape's structure.

OTES

rawing notes is a beneficial activity for all artists. For the atercolor artist, the note is a way of capturing a fresh and ontaneous representation of a theme from nature that can painted later in the studio. The painter cannot venture it into the countryside loaded down with materials. We are it to discover an interesting landscape when we have othing to draw with. It is not essential to carry too many ings around with you—paper and a pencil are enough. hen we say paper, we actually mean a small sketch pad at you can carry in your pocket. The pencil should be soft facilitate rapid drawing and shading.

The notes we accumulate on our strolls through the coun-yside are useful for suggesting a composition or point of ew; they can be combined for a painting in the studio, and me of them may even have artistic value in themselves. It useful to carry a drawing pad around with you, even when you are about to embark on a painting, since it allows you to try out new viewpoints or details while you are working.

COLOR NOTES

Certain watercolor manufactur-ers sell miniature, pocket-size sets of watercolors and a small brush, specially designed for painting notes in color. They enable us to combine our pen-cil drawings with some color indications. You can attach a small plastic container to your paint set for carrying water.

COLOR MIXTURES

These are the basic color mixtures that were used to paint this landscape. As you can see, the blues are not the only color— sienna, orange, carmine, and greens all contribute to creating a range of interesting grays. The mixtures at the bottom of this page correspond with the vegetation and earth of the pain ing. The lesson to be learned here is to always search out t variety and wealth of color by mixing. Two shades of gree are better than one.

MAKING A CARDBOARD FRAME

To make your own cardboard frame, cut out two right-angle strips of black card, about 1¼" wide, each strip measuring about 8" in length. Use sturdy cardboard, to prevent it from twisting. If you want to use it to frame a composition, simply stick the two pieces together with adhesive tape.

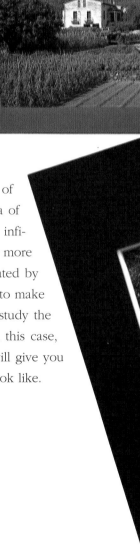

THE FIT

To "fit," or frame, the subject is one way of composing the motif. This gives you an idea of what it will look like on paper. There are an infinite number of different shapes, but some are more attractive than others. The fit is always dictated by the size and format of the paper. It is useful to make a cardboard frame through which you can study the framing of the subject before painting it. In this case, make it the same size as your paper. This will give you a general idea of what the watercolor will look like.

MOUNTAIN LANDSCAPE

*O*ur first exercise consists of capturing the clear and fresh colors of this marvelous mountain scene. It is obvious that the photograph was taken on a spring day: Everything is clean, clear, and very cold. We will therefore have to use clearly separated clean colors, adjusting to the limits imposed by the lines of the drawing. The brightness of the snow on the mountains will provide us with the opportunity to practice a common watercolor technique: reserving the white of the paper. This is a relatively simple method that, as you are about to see, produces very convincing results. Without further ado, let's get down to work.

MATERIALS

- Cold-pressed 16" × 20" watercolor paper
- Stick of charcoal
- Sable or ox-hair brushes numbers 4, 10, and 14
- Synthetic fiber 3/4"–1 1/4" brush
- Large synthetic 2"–2 3/4" brush
- Selection of the tubes of watercolors on the preceding pages
- Palette box with wells for holding the paints

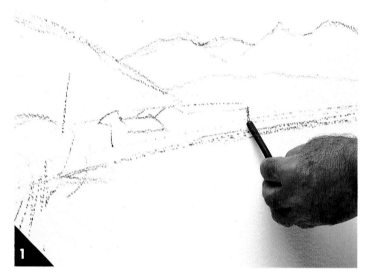

1 Our composition is iden tical to the photograph so we have sketched in th scene in the same propo tions. This charcoal drawin contains only the basi lines, the essential ones tha we will use as a guide.

2 Using an ultramarin blue wash, we paint th sky and outline it along th ridge of the mountai range. It should be pur ultramarine, with no othe color added, and withou sudden light or dark grada tions. The sky should pos sess the clear bright unifor color that is so characteristi of this type of landscape.

PAINTING A MOUNTAIN LANDSCAPE

The hills in the middle ground were painted with a mixture of sap green and a touch of burnt sienna, a dark and very saturated mix, which was applied with loose brushstrokes.

The houses of the village were painted with flat colors of different light and dark tones, working within the same range of browns, but leaving some areas of clean white paper.

Despite their apparently complex appearance, the mountains were painted very freely, running the tip of the brush over the lightly dampened paper.

The sky consists of lightly diluted ultramarine blue applied in a wash that lightens as it approaches the horizon until it blends with the white of the snow.

These shrubs are mixtures of ochre, sienna, and carmine. The brushstrokes and the color mixtures are visible, as is the darkened area at the bottom, produced by the addition of raw umber. The trunks were suggested by painting several brushstrokes of clean water.

The yellow flowers transform the top of the hill into a mass of yellow, which was painted with a large wide brush. In the lower part, the yellow alternates with green. The speckled effect of the flowers was achieved by flicking the brush loaded with paint onto the paper.

3 We are dampening the mountains with water so that when we come to paint them, the color will lighten and blend easily. The dark mountain on the left is painted with a mix of very diluted dark green and sienna.

4 Here you can see the clean, white paper in the form of the houses. This white area must be outlined with great care, because we have to go around the shape in the same way that we would draw it.

THE DAMPNESS OF THE PAPER

The results of working on damp paper and on dry paper are very different. On dry paper the brushstrokes remain clearly visible and unpainted white areas are easy to leave. On damp paper the brushstrokes blend into each other and spread more evenly, and it is difficult, if not impossible, to leave unpainted areas or to outline forms.

5 Using the wider brush we paint the open space in pure cadmium yellow pale. The wide brush ensures that the area will appear clean and free of brushstrokes.

6 At the bottom of the hill we have applied some yellowish green unevenly diluted in water to obtain the effect of mottled grass, which is painted in by working alternately with a very dry brush and a very damp one.

7 We are varying the green with some very diluted yellow, which heightens the mottled effect and helps to suggest the flowers. Nonetheless, the effect must be reinforced further still. Using a brush loaded with green, we paint the small patches of grass that can be seen among the yellow of the flowers.

8 Let's start painting the mountain range. We moistened the paper earlier, so it still retains a certain amount of dampness. This allows us to easily lighten the color as it approaches the snow-capped peaks.

9 The mountain range is finished. We have used the same technique on all the peaks: painting with the tip of the brush on damp paper, leaving a few white areas to indicate the volume of the rocky masses.

10 It is easy to suggest the speckled effect of the flowers in the foreground. With a brush loaded with yellow, we flick the paint onto the paper.

11 Apart from the houses of the village, the rest of our picture is almost complete. We are using a very simple technique: Each area is assigned its own particular color and treatment. This technique lends the painting a clear and bright finish, worthy of the cold atmosphere of the day. It is useful to pause and consider such aspects so as not to lose sight of the work as a whole.

12 Now we are concentrating on the buildings. Using flat planes of color, we build the houses as if they were boxes, thus giving them shape and volume. Some parts of the paper are left white to indicate the snow and sunlight on the walls.

13 The houses are painted in ochre and siennas intensified with bluish grays to obtain the contrast of the shadows. The branches of the trees that can be seen in front of one of the houses were painted with strokes of clean water over the dark green of the mountains.

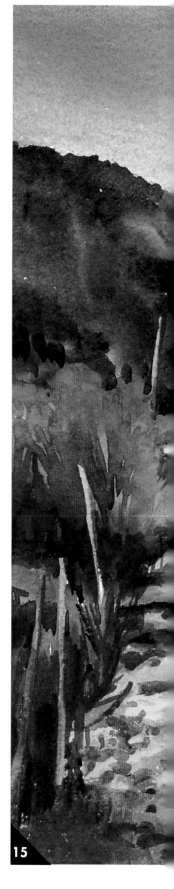

CHOOSING THE CORRECT BRUSH

As we have seen, different types of brushes produce different types of finishes. Wide brushes cover broad areas with a uniform color. Round brushes are good for washes, loose brushwork, and details. It is possible to do everything with a single brush, but the results tend to appear monotonous.

14 By constructing the houses as if they were boxes and distributing the lights and shadows of the walls appropriately, we have managed to depict the village with relative ease.

15 The watercolor is finished. Our objective was a clean painting with strong contrasts, an effect that accurately reflects the cold clear day of the scene.

PAINTING A CLOUDY LANDSCAPE

*W*e *return to the mountain theme in this second exercise, only this time the range is seen from a distance, from a perspective that includes a wide valley through which a river runs. The landscape is dominated by the presence of low storm clouds, which tint the entire panorama with a grayish tone. This tonality is the key to this watercolor, which we will paint on damp paper, allowing the colors to spread more freely.*

1 We drew the sketch in charcoal. Just as in the first exercise, our sketch includes only the most important lines, which situate the different planes, indicate the height of the horizon, and distribute the cloudy masses on the sky.

MATERIALS

- Cold-pressed 16" × 20" watercolor paper
- Stick of charcoal
- Sable or ox-hair brushes numbers 4, 10, and 14
- Synthetic fiber ³/₄"–1¹/₄" brush
- Large synthetic 2–2³/₄" brush
- Tubes of watercolors in our usual selection of colors
- Natural sponge
- Cloths or absorbent paper towels
- Palette box with wells for holding the paints

2 We are going to paint the sky on damp paper. First we run the cloth over the surface to remove any excess charcoal, and then we lightly rub a damp sponge over the area of the sky. To avoid leaving any drops of water on the paper we must make sure that the sponge is only damp.

The background gray of the sky was obtained with ultramarine blue and burnt sienna, applied with a wide brush on the damp surface of the paper, thus allowing the color to spread freely.

The darkest area of the mass of cloud was obtained by applying dense sky colors over a damp base, with the gray hues brought out by rubbing with a brush.

The sky clears and the clouds thin out in the area nearest the horizon. This was painted with a very soft and transparent wash, applied on wet paper, which barely tints the paper.

The chestnut tones of the hills were applied with generously diluted brushstrokes. In fact, the entire lower part of the watercolor was painted with sweeping brushstrokes.

The green strips that represent the trees were worked over the color of the hill while it was still damp. The important point is to ensure that these details "explain" the shape of the hill.

The peak of this mountain plays an important role in giving the panorama depth. The dark and cool shades create contrast with both the sky (also cool but lighter) and the nearer mountains (painted in warm shades).

3 We begin by painting the sky with a mixture of blue and burnt sienna, to which we add a touch of burnt umber to gray the tone. Since the paper is damp, there is no need to concentrate too much on ensuring that the color covers and spreads. The dampness of the paper will provide the color with an interesting texture.

3

4 Once we have covered the dark part of the sky, we can start to intensify the darkest clouds by going over the painted area with a mixture of the same color. Here we have to work over a half-dry color because we want to avoid sharply defined limits.

5 Here we can see the cloudiest part of the sky completely painted. The varying qualities and shades of color are visible thanks to the dampness of the paper and the different amounts of water that we have used.

6 To paint the lower part of the sky, we apply a gray wash diluted with abundant water. This will be the base over which we will tone and give pictorial life to the transparencies of the horizon.

WORKING WITH ABUNDANT WATER

Using abundant water when painting in watercolor, moistening the paper, and applying washes and mixtures of color is very pleasant because the effects appear to emerge on their own. Nonetheless, do not overdo it, because the shapes tend to blur and it is very difficult to predict the final result.

7 The work in this part of the sky must be delicate; we have to exploit the transparencies, with very diluted tones and shades of color. The blue cloud that you can see on the right softly highlights the clear sky, thus lending the landscape depth.

8 We paint the farthest mountains with a very dark blue-gray, which contrasts with the light area of the sky and creates a visual center of interest. This new contrast also heightens the sense of depth. We do not paint these mountains until the color we applied beforehand has completely dried; only in this way is it possible to clearly define the contours, which otherwise would blend with the dampness of the sky.

9 The most important aspect of this exercise is the color contrast created between the bluish grays (very cool colors) and the siennas and umbers (warm colors). The warm colors, those in the nearest mountains, are what we are going to paint now. They will help us to define the shape of the mountains.

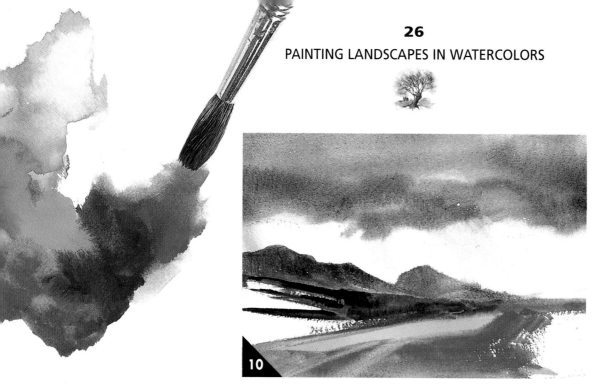

10 We are using th warmer colors (sie nas and carmines) of o palette to represent the field The mixture of these two co ors produces a chestnut ton which we dilute with wat and apply to model the ligh and shadows of the mou tains. We accomplish the tas with plenty of water, allow ing the paint to spread, with out attempting details.

THE TONE OF A LANDSCAPE

Even in the most colorful picture there is a predominating tone, which may be cool, warm, or intermixed. This does not mean that all the colors of the painting should resemble one another; rather, they should capture the climate or atmosphere of the landscape, which implies highlighting certain color ranges and not others. In this case, we are using slightly muted colors.

11 The volume of the mountains in the foreground, which we have constructed with varying densities of color, is almost complete. We paint ochre in the highlighted areas to suggest the effect of light filtering through the clouds.

12 The entire surface of the paper is now covered with paint, which means the tone has been established. It is an intermixed tone, that is to say, a neutral one, with a gray tendency, which depicts the ashy luminosity of the sky.

13 We begin now to fill in the scene with trees and vegetation, beginning with the row of trees, which we paint in a very dense sap green. We paint while the base color is still damp enough for us to lightly blend the brushstrokes into the chestnut tonality.

14 The weather is unpredictable; we don't know whether the clouds are about to unleash sheets of rain or the sun will appear between them. In this situation it is essential to work quickly to capture the general tone of the landscape. Otherwise you may lose the atmosphere, and the resulting watercolor will appear confusing, with an unlikely mix of lights. If we get the atmosphere on the paper in time, everything else will be easier, because afterward it is merely a job of painting in the details on a correctly harmonized background.

15 We darken some of the mountain faces to intensify their volume. This darkening is obtained by painting a thin layer of sienna on a completely dry color, with a wide synthetic brush.

BRUSHWORK

In addition to the color, the brushstroke is important: its width, its direction, its capacity to suggest a shape, etc. Brushstrokes can construct the composition and recreate the atmosphere. Each subject requires individual treatment: soft strokes, energetic strokes, careful strokes for detailing, etc. You can practice these different strokes by painting abstract lines on a sheet of paper.

16 We have included a few trees on the hills in the form of a number of specks. They lend a sense of perspective, which distances the viewer from the landscape and the shape of the hills and mountains.

17 The breadth of the view lends the finished watercolor a monumental appearance: The mountains and hills are seen in all their splendor thanks to the trees represented by specks of paint that scale the landscape down to size. The dramatic quality of the sky is balanced by the chestnut-colored fields.

PAINTING TREES AND A RIVER

*W*ater *is a common theme in watercolor landscapes. This exercise consists of painting a river
from the bank. Although it is not colorful, this
scene is rich in nuances of color, the general intonation
being a grayish green. This exercise will deal especially with
the application of shadings and the direction of the stroke,
the latter of which is a vital factor for capturing the surface
of the river.*

MATERIALS

• Cold-pressed 16" × 20"
watercolor paper
• Stick of charcoal
• Sable or ox-hair brushes
numbers 4, 10, and 14
• Synthetic fiber ³/₄"–1¹/₄"
brush
• Tubes of watercolors, especially siennas, ochres, umbers,
and greens
• Cloths or absorbent paper
towels
• Palette box with wells for
holding the paints

1 We start by drawing. A
usual, we sketch th
general shapes of the mo
important objects. In th
case the picture require
more attention than usua
due to the compositiona
importance of the tre
trunks. We create volume b
blending the charcoal wit
our fingers.

2 After cleaning the
surface of the paper
with a cloth to remove any
excess charcoal, we begin to
paint. Maybe you are surprised by
the way we start, since first we paint the
trees that appear farthest away in the landscape in sienna and green. The reason for this
is that these two colors establish the general values in the
painting.

PAINTING TREES AND A RIVER

he light falling on one side of e trunk, which creates an tense chiaroscuro, or contrast light and shade, was obtained ith a long stroke of clear water ver dark sienna and carmine.

The wooded area on the far bank has been painted directly over a dry background. The three-dimensional quality of the treetops is achieved by superimposing thick strokes of sap green with sienna and carmine.

The color of the sky is the white of the paper. The day is overcast, and the light-colored clouds are spread over the sky.

The effect of the leaves against the light was easy to achieve. We applied several touches of ochre and green on the white sky with the tip of the brush. It was essential to observe the leaves carefully to get the effect right.

he dark areas of the water are ch in transparencies and lended color. The contrast etween khaki or neutral ochre nd the dark green is one of the eys.

Here are the mixtures of color and transparencies, as well as the clean white paper that represents the lightest areas of the water, in which the sky is reflected.

3 We continue painting the treetops. We use ochre, over which we paint sap green, creating a cold and wintery con- ast, which begins to define the general color of the picture.

4 We are now finishing off the trees along the bank, con- tinuing with very dark sap green and ochre. To create the hapes of these trees is not as difficult as it seems. It is all ased on brushwork. The outline of the treetops is the result f applying brushstrokes that create the branches and foliage itting out.

4

5 There is no need to change water to paint the shadows of the trees on the surface of the water; it is enough to follow the directions of the reflections marked by the still-visible strokes of the original drawing, painting loose strokes, without overworking or retouching. The effect of the movement of the water is the result of light, careful brushstrokes.

6 The shadows cast on the river by the trees are muc more uniform that the trees themselves. The colors use for the shadows are homogeneous, just suggesting th foliage, and the brushstrokes are careful and even.

7 When the first color has dried, we add a few strokes bluish gray, a mixture of sap green and ultramarine blu which suggest movement on the surface of the water an create a horizontal plane.

8 The watercolor is at an advanced stage. Here we can see the progress we have made in the reflections on the water. Light grays have been to added to harmonize the dark areas of the shadows with the highlights. They are painted using the lines of the original drawing as a guide.

9 The trees are painted with successive thin layers of reddish gray, which are very light at the beginning, and then darkened (in the tree on the left) until an almost black tone is attained. The lighter side of the tree is obtained by running a brush loaded with water down the side, to lift the color.

10 Here we see how the trunks are worked to obtain their cylindrical shape. We have intensified the color over an area of clear water. Over the resulting dark color, we create the highlight reflected on the trunk with a brush loaded with clean water.

PAINTING REFLECTIONS

Painting reflections on a river, a lake, or a sea can be a thrilling experience, especially if we understand all the possibilities that the watercolor medium has to offer. Observation is important in this respect: seeing and understanding the rhythm of the waves and ripples on the surface of the water. Once you have grasped this and know what colors you require to paint water, it is relatively simple to obtain the loose and liquid effect of the water.

11 We can see that the reflections on the water consist of green-ochre, khaki, bluish green, and very light gray. The secret lies in the gradation from dark to light, taking care that the direction of the brushstrokes expresses the delicate ripple movement on the surface.

12 The only addition here is the earth in the foreground, a mix of burnt sienna and carmine. This plane plays a vital role in defining the distance between the foreground and the far bank of the composition, and produces a color contrast with respect to the picture as a whole.

13 The treatment of the reflections has made this a particularly challenging exercise. Apart from the need to observe and study the direction and rhythm of the ripples, you should not find any serious problems with this watercolor.

PAINTING A TRACK THROUGH A SNOW-COVERED FOREST

*S*now is a subject that looks best in watercolors. As you saw in the first exercise, it is relatively easy to "paint" snow by leaving the paper clean and unpainted. There is more snow in this painting than in that of the first exercise, and most importantly, it is close to the viewer. For this reason we are going to have to shade it and refine it much more than on the first occasion.

MATERIALS

- Cold-pressed 16" × 20" watercolor paper
- Stick of charcoal
- Sable or ox-hair brushes numbers 4, 10, and 14
- Synthetic fiber ³/₄"–1¹/₄" brush
- Large synthetic 2"–2³/₄" brush
- Tubes of watercolors, especially burnt sienna, raw umber, ultramarine blue, carmine, and ochre
- Cloths or absorbent paper towels
- Palette box with wells for holding the paints

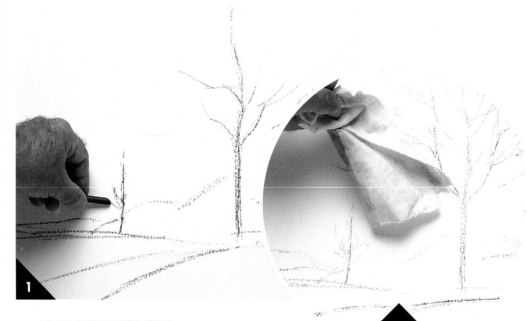

1 First we draw a preliminary sketch and mark out the masses of the lan scape. We locate the horizon line and the verticals of t post, on the left, and the tree, on the right.

2 Once the initial composition has been drawn, we r the cloth over the paper to remove any excess charco It is important not to rub too hard; just lightly run the cl a couple of times over the paper, as if you were dusting with a feather.

3 We are going to begin painting with the sky. Once ag we will paint on a dampened area with a wide brush the edge of the drawing, marked by the trees on the h zon. This we will do with a very watered-down, alm dirty, gray, the definitive color of the sky.

PAINTING A TRACK THROUGH A SNOW-COVERED FOREST

The sky is almost white, since it was painted with a very watery gray. The effect of the white clouds was created with a wash containing some extremely subtle gray tones.

The leaves of the trees were painted with brown washes diluted with varying amounts of water. These leaves form a screen of semitransparent color over which the branches stand out.

The tree trunks and branches were painted with a blackish tone, composed of carmine, blue, and raw umber. The work is more akin to drawing (using the tip of the brush) than painting.

The darker bushes contain the same colors as the branches, only in this case they were more diluted and varied. Subtle nuances of value and hue can be observed.

The trees farthest away were painted with a very transparent gray wash, very freely, avoiding details or retouching. It is the wash itself that defines and determines the shape, profile, and volume of these trees.

The snow was suggested by leaving the paper white and then adding washes in some areas. Carefully placed brushstrokes of very diluted gray cross over one another and become superimposed, creating the volume of the snow-covered earth.

4 These brushstrokes correspond to the trees on the horizon. The color used is a mixture of burnt sienna and just a touch of raw umber to neutralize the tone. The direction of the brushstrokes also defines the shape of the trees.

5 Painting on dampened paper creates an especially soft color. The brushstrokes blend into each other, so the shapes come together in masses of similar tones that evoke mist. With a lightly loaded brush, we gradually construct the trees, painting successive layers of color, allowing the brushstrokes to run over the dampness of the paper.

6 We gradually darken the color, adding tones, painting with a slightly more loaded brush. Due to their proximity, the bushes on the right appear darker, an effect obtained by applying very lightly diluted burnt umber.

7 It is interesting to see the effects produced by the different techniques: the trees painted on wet paper, and the ground painted on dry paper. They make the earth appear much starker and heighten the contrast to the whiteness of the snow on the ground. Hard and soft contrasts complement each other, adding visual interest to watercolor paintings.

8 We reserved several large areas for the snow earlier on. Now it is time to paint them with very diluted brushstrokes of gray to create relief. It is important not to apply the strokes in a rigorous fashion; they must be painted loosely and resolutely. It is only in this way that we can evoke a convincing suggestion of the unevenness of the terrain. Make sure you don't cover the entire white surface because this would muddy it. Our brushstrokes must be viewed as white shadows.

PAINTING SNOW

In watercolor, white is provided by the white of the paper, because there is no white paint. Therefore, to paint snow, we have to leave areas of paper unpainted, and then tone them later. These tones must be extremely subtle so as not to ruin the white effect. If they are done correctly, the white will appear as a real color instead of as an unpainted fragment of the paper.

9 We have diluted the gray strokes over the snow by running a damp brush over them; this action turns the grays into lighter and more transparent tones that shade the white of the snow without spoiling or lessening the strong contrast of the white paper against the dark carmine tones.

10 We are painting the trunk and the branches of the tree with burnt sienna, using the tip of the brush. This is more like drawing than painting, since we are using the lines of the initial drawing as a guide, as well as our observation of the tree itself.

11 The shape of the tree is completed. We can appreciate the combination of darker and lighter tones and shades, as if the tree were shrouded in mist. This effect has been achieved thanks to working on damp paper and to the contrast of the lines of the branches.

12 It is interesting to experiment with the effects of the blurred outlines that are produced by the dampness of the paper and the short brushstrokes. This small tree has been painted on a dry background. Its dark leaves stand out against the snow and, at the same time, are lost and fade into the background.

13 We continue highlighting the branches, working, as always, with the tip of the brush. The strokes should be consistent with the shape and disposition of the washes representing the treetops, no matter how blended or toned down the painting may be after the paper has dried.

THE USEFULNESS OF A TOWEL

When you are working with water, and the painting requires work with washes, it is essential to have an old clean towel handy for removing some or all of the water from the brush. A towel is also useful for removing excess paint from a brush, as well as for drying the paper when it is too wet.

14 The picture is almost finished; all that remains to be done is to develop the trees on the right. With respect to harmony, it is interesting to note we have obtained a considerable wealth of values and tones from very few colors, in accordance with the general neutral aspect of the landscape. This is a good exercise for working with color and for practice in painting on both wet and dry paper.

15 Our work on the branches is ever more complex, since we must intensify the tone with successive brushstrokes. The objective is to obtain a strong contrast between the trunks and branches and the leaves and snow in the background.

16 Again we can observe the wealth of different tonal intensities. It is worth mentioning the fact that these different intensities by themselves create depth: the softer they are, the farther away the washes appear. This is an important factor in a landscape dominated by mist or fog.

17 Another interesting effect obtained in this watercolor is the number of small green strokes on the left, which break the monotony of the umber tones, incorporating a cool and dark accent that perfectly harmonizes within the whole. One can sense the cold and damp atmosphere of the scene thanks to contrasts such as these.

KNOWING WHEN TO STOP

In watercolor paintings it is easy to lay down washes, transparencies, and strokes of color, which are applied according to the rhythm of the work and the appeal of their effects. It is important to know when to stop and not overdo these techniques, otherwise you will end up ruining the harmony of the painting and hardening the shapes. It is vital to recognize when a painting is finished, and the moment when the effect you are striving for is obtained.

18 The treetops are becoming denser and richer in tone with each successive addition of color. These layers are almost always the same: raw umber applied in varying degrees of intensity and in successive transparent layers.

19 Over the whites and pale grays of the snow, we have applied several touches of umber to suggest those parts of the ground that are not covered in snow. The small details are the important ones because they bring the picture to life.

20 As a final touch, we blend any color that is still damp by rubbing it with our fingers. This should be carried out only when the color is almost completely dry. Otherwise the shape of the wash may be ruined and, maybe, the paper itself.

21 The exercise is complete. It is interesting from a technical point of view because of the washes and the narrow color range. The foggy, cold, and damp winter atmosphere has been correctly painted.

PAINTING A COMPOSITION CENTERED ON A TREE

*W*e are now going to try a different composition. Instead of painting a panoramic scene, we are going to concentrate on just one element of a landscape: a tree. A theme like this should be treated the same way as you would treat a figure—that is to say, it should be painted on a vertical format. This exercise will demonstrate how it is possible to paint a less conventional landscape with a monumental effect and a centralized shape, two relatively rare aspects in this genre.

MATERIALS
- Cold-pressed 16" x 20" watercolor paper
- Stick of charcoal
- Sable or ox-hair brushes numbers 4, 10, and 14
- Synthetic fiber ³/₄"–1¹/₄" brush
- Tubes of watercolors, especially greens, yellows, oranges, carmine, and siennas
- Cloths or absorbent paper towels
- Palette box with wells for holding the paints

The sky was painted with a very diluted blue wash. We painted from top to bottom, gradually adding more water. For this reason the top part of the sky is darker than the lower part.

The crown of this pine tree was treated with strong contrasts of green, which were obtained by superimposing several layers while working with very thick color. The darkest washes contain carmine, which turns them almost black.

This small tree was done in the negative, painting around the edge with a very dark tone (a mix of sap green and carmine) to make the treetop stand out clearly against the darkness of the trees in the background.

1 First we make a complete and detailed drawing of the subject. Pay special attention to the curves and bends of the branches from the very start because they are important aspects of this tree.

2 We apply the first shades of green, in this case a yellowish green, which we use to paint large areas of the background. Then, using a blue wash, we paint the sky in the same way.

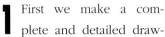

We obtain this greenish yellow ochre from a mixture of yellow and a touch of green, which we use to paint the light areas of the leaves and the tree trunk. Here we are working on dry paper but with enough water to allow the brushstrokes to flow freely.

The trunk and the branches were painted with a rather light yellow wash as a base, over which we added several dark strokes and touches of a mix of orange and carmine to represent the bark. The resulting reddish tone creates a light contrast with the basically green tone of the painting.

The contrast between the ground and the background of the forest is represented here by a line that cuts the continuity of the color. The tone was darkened considerably above this line to create a visual effect of distance between the two planes.

The road provides a powerful perspective that leads the foreground into the background. The areas without grass were painted with a violet-gray wash; the curved shape of the tracks of the road also suggests the shape of a hill that gives way to the middle ground of the composition.

4 We apply new washes of green over the first wash and partially blend them in. The shape and volume begin to emerge thanks to the first touches. The contrast of light and dark that we are creating also accentuates the shape of the tree trunk.

5 The darkest details of the branches and leaves are depicted with washes and strokes of uniform color. The unevenness of the washes (seen in the lower right-hand part of the crown of the pine tree) is interpreted by the viewer as details. Instead of copying them, it is sufficient to suggest them in such a simple and effective way as this.

6 This is the negative treatment of the small pine tree. We paint around the tree with a very dark mixture of carmine and sap green. Once the outer shape is defined, we can paint the interior with a lighter color.

7 We are advancing quickly, creating a feeling of three dimensions with an abundance of green contrasts. The low hills are represented with brushstrokes in different directions.

8 By holding the brush at the end, with the wrist slightly twisted, we obtain loose brushstrokes that are particularly suitable for depicting the lightest branches, working with very diluted color.

HOLDING THE BRUSH

The most common way to hold the brush is just like a pencil, only farther from the brush end, making it easy to control the movement and allowing a certain amount of freedom. To paint sweeping and more undefined brush-strokes, the brush should be held far from the brush end, painting with a slack wrist. Holding the brush too near to the hairs reduces manual dexterity.

The sensation of distance between the central pine tree and the trees in the background has been achieved, and the only job remaining is to finish the foreground.

10 The day is gray but bright. It is a pleasure to paint on days like this because there are no changes in light intensity, the tones do not alter, and the contrasts between light and shadow are constant and stable, thus enabling us to work calmly.

11 The curved brushstrokes in the foreground follow the shape of the road. This series of curves creates the hi. in the foreground and, at the same time, creates the effec of perspective, since instead of being parallel, the curve converge.

12 The darkening tones of the road and the low hill ove which it runs also reinforce the sensation of distanc from the area where the pine tree stands, which is muc lighter in comparison.

13 Our picture is almost complete. Note how the contrasts between the tones of green suggest the shapes and create the effect of their advancing or receding in space according to the rhythm of the composition and the direction of the light.

14 The exercise is con plete. This is a fin demonstration of how landscape containing on single element can posses its own artistic merit, with out the necessity of integra ing it into a more comple composition. A tree, as yo can see, is a world in itse of tones and lights tha deserve to be treated wit the same care as the mo: beautiful of panoramas.

PAINTING SNOW-COVERED PEAKS AT DUSK

*S*now is once again the subject of our exercise, this time with a marvelous pink and blue tonality. As you can see, snow has an infinite number of pictorial possibilities, especially in watercolor. Snow is the white surface of the paper, and the subtle tonalities of a snowy-covered landscape can be represented by transparencies that are best achieved with watercolor. This landscape comprises chromatic colors that cannot escape the watercolor artist unnoticed. Let's get down to work and see if we can reflect the special charm of these colors.

MATERIALS

- Cold-pressed 16" × 20" watercolor paper
- Stick of charcoal
- Sable or ox-hair brushes numbers 4, 10, and 14
- Synthetic fiber ³/₄"–1¹/₄" brush
- Tubes of watercolors, especially yellows, siennas, oranges, blues, and carmines
- Cloths or absorbent paper towels
- Palette box with wells for holding the paints

1 The composition is extremely simple—the range of mountains crosses the paper horizontally in a soft wavy line. The peaks separate the three main planes: The foreground is the rocks, the middle ground is the snow-covered mountains, and the background is the sky.

2 We are including a few details in the first sketch, such as the snow caps, some jutting edges of rocks, and the unevenness of the lower area of the mountain range. As usual, after finishing the charcoal sketch, we remove the dust and clean the paper with a cloth.

The clouds were painted wet on wet paper, applying very diluted carmine and a touch of grayish blue to obtain the soft cottony effect.

The quality of the light at this time of the afternoon gives a yellow hue to the illuminated part of the snow. It is precisely this quality that lends the tones a pinkish transparent tendency.

The shadows cast on the snow are transparent. They were painted with a very diluted wash, without any sharp contrasts or abrupt endings. We used free brushwork to create these shadows.

The blue of the sky is a wash of uniform intensity, worked with wide sweeping strokes, blending one into another, using a wide synthetic brush on damp paper.

This is the contrast necessary to pull all the tones of the picture together. A very dark umber was applied in broad strokes, with the brush abundantly loaded with water and paint. This wash contains no details but is not a smooth surface either; since it presents different intensities within the same hue.

This strip of snow in shadow was neutralized by grays applied on dry paper, with a color diluted with only a small amount of water. Since we worked with dry brushstrokes, the grain of the paper remains visible, creating an expressive texture of a snowy quality.

3 Let's begin with the clouds. With our brush abundantly loaded with water and very diluted carmine, we paint several soft forms with diffuse contours.

3

4 Water plays an important role in the first
stages of the work, and all
the colors of the sky are
heavily diluted. To keep control of these damp areas, we
have to work slowly, without
blending all the colors.

5 Once the blues and th
pinks have been applie
in their appropriate places
we can soften their edge
with a damp brush and cre
ate blended areas.

6 Now we are paintin
the illuminated faces o
the mountains. Continuin
with the soft warm tonality
we apply several areas o
very transparent yellov
containing a lot of wate
The sky appears to be com
plete and its brightness ha
to be continued in th
mountains.

CREATING TONALITIES

Working within a warm range
does not necessarily mean
that you have to make use of
warm colors in all their intensities. We can create varying
warm tonalities by working
with very diluted colors, creating contrasts, blends, transparencies, and so on. The
addition of a cool color helps
to give relief and life to the
warmth of the whole.

This large area of paint defines the area of snow in shadow. It is neither a uniform color nor a series of tones: ~~c~~armine and blue make up the general color, lightened with ~~w~~ater. The darkest area of shadow is represented by medium ~~bl~~ue blended into areas as a whole.

Having painted the faces of the mountain in shadow, we begin to construct the huge contrasting shadow toward the bottom of the picture, ~~w~~here we paint a thick ~~ap~~plication of dark umber, ~~m~~ixed with carmine, over ~~th~~e pink area (allowing the ~~p~~ink to dry first in order to ~~av~~oid having the colors run ~~an~~d become muddy).

We have kept the lower part of the paper clean, ~~w~~orking around it with great ~~p~~recision. It outlines the ~~sh~~ape of the mountain in the ~~fo~~reground. It is essential to ~~al~~low the first washes on the ~~sk~~y and mountains to dry ~~th~~oroughly before painting ~~th~~e foreground so that we can ~~av~~oid blurring the contours.

10 We are painting the mountain face in shadow with brush loaded with color, without too much water. W have avoided using a lot of water in the area of snow on th right, since its relative dryness has left the texture of th grain of the paper visible.

11 The softness of the tonality does not mean we do not use a wealth of color. This detail shows how a variety of very different tones can be brought together in a single harmony. The pure sienna that can be seen on the far left is a snowless peak that is brightened by reflected sunlight.

12 Although we have been working with abundant water, blending colors and softening forms, we have not lost the underlying structure. The washes are used to represent the volume of the faces of the mountain; the sharp contrasts of the dark umber reinforce this effect.

13 The contrast of th foreground has bee achieved. It is thanks to th contrast that the delica tones of the snow-covere faces are highlighted an emphasized in all their pict rial splendor. As you ca see, this exercise is, abov all, a lesson in color ha mony; the drawing disap pears and makes way for th color, and it is through col that form must be expresse

14 There has been a significant change here. The pinks and mauves that shade the snow-covered sides have been darkened with a very diluted raw umber wash, which has unified the previously applied hues into a cooler and more solid unit, more appropriate to the motif.

CONSERVING QUALITIES

When we work with abundant water, creating blends and transparencies, mixing directly on the paper, accidents can and do happen—that is to say, we create unpredicted effects and qualities. These qualities can be interesting and may even be worth retaining. In such cases, random chance is on our side, creating forms and colors that would have been difficult to concoct deliberately.

15 The face of the mountain on the far right has been treated with several sienna washes to depict the rocks and the crest. These washes add interest to the entire mountain face in shadow, heightening the contrast with the parts of lighted snow. We have applied these touches with a very dry brush.

16 We now turn our attention to the rocks in the foreground and outline them with a very thick color using a dry brush. They had become blurred when we dampened the dark faces with an umber-colored wash.

17 We have added several small touches and strokes of very dark umber on top of the dry wash. These applications give the panorama size and scale, creating distance and allowing the dimensions of these great mountain faces to be fully appreciated.

THE SCALE OF THE WHOLE

When painting distant landscapes, such as mountains or the sea, it is difficult to do justice to the dimension. The mountains may appear to be minute. It is essential, therefore, to include some small details, such as rocks, trees, and so on, to serve as an indication of the real scale of the scene. This kind of work should be left to last.

18 This area, the most complex part of the watercolor, is now complete. The contrast between the foreground and the rest is solid and well defined, and the brightness follows a gradual ascension, from the very dark lower area to the light of the sky. The lower part of the snow-covered peaks has volume, and we have managed to express the rocky outcroppings through color.

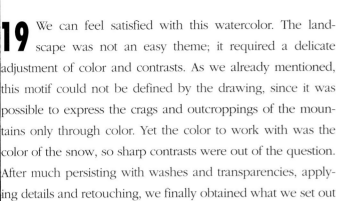

19 We can feel satisfied with this watercolor. The landscape was not an easy theme; it required a delicate adjustment of color and contrasts. As we already mentioned, this motif could not be defined by the drawing, since it was possible to express the crags and outcroppings of the mountains only through color. Yet the color to work with was the color of the snow, so sharp contrasts were out of the question. After much persisting with washes and transparencies, applying details and retouching, we finally obtained what we set out to paint and, at the same time, gained invaluable experience.

PAINTING A LANDSCAPE FROM AN ELEVATED POINT OF VIEW

*T*he main interest of this last exercise is the elevated point of view chosen. The horizon is at the top edge of the paper, and there are multiple planes between the foreground and the distant valley, passing through a series of hills and mounds. This is not an especially difficult theme, but it all depends on your finding the right composition.

MATERIALS

- Cold-pressed 16" × 20" watercolor paper
- Stick of charcoal
- Sable or ox-hair brushes numbers 4, 10, and 14
- Synthetic fiber 3/4"–1 1/4" brush
- Tubes of watercolors, especially greens, ochres, yellows, siennas, and blues
- Cloths or absorbent paper towels
- Palette box with wells for holding the paints

1 The sketch is quite detailed, emphasizing the directional lines of the composition. Diagonal lines suggest the depth of the landscape. We sketched this drawing with simplified straight lines; only the tree contain a few simple curve to outline their genera shape. It is not necessary to add details, since we will be doing this as we progress.

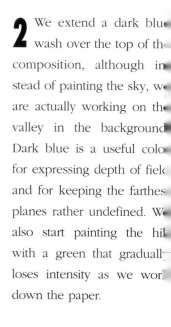

2 We extend a dark blue wash over the top of the composition, although in stead of painting the sky, we are actually working on the valley in the background Dark blue is a useful colo for expressing depth of field and for keeping the farthes planes rather undefined. We also start painting the hill with a green that graduall loses intensity as we work down the paper.

he horizon and the sky are visible only in this corner. This small fragment is enough to interpret the rest of the dark blue area as fields in the distance.

The mountains in the background were painted in a dark tone, although no significant details were included. They were not necessary, since the watercolor already has an abundance of details.

These trees mark the unevenness between the plane on which the farm buildings stand and the mountains in the background. The trees were given individual colors and shapes.

The light areas of vegetation are crops on the plain. They were painted with heavily diluted wash, without any changes of color or texture to break their continuity.

he work on this treetop was carried out by alternating broad washes and individual brush-strokes. This gives the sensation of movement, which allows the effect of light through the leaves.

The farmhouse was painted with quite a lot of detail, emphasizing both the effect of light and shadow produced by the openings in the façade and the umber hues of the roof.

3 We continue painting from top to bottom, bringing the color masses down, leaving the branches of the trees white, painting very diluted ochre washes that express the horizontal breadth of the fields, always following our compositional lines.

4 One fragment is now completed. We worked quickly, alternating dark strokes on light damp washes. It is interesting to note how the blurry contours create a feeling of distance.

5 We are now working on the branches of the tree that we left unpainted. We paint a solid opaque area using a rather dry brush, leaving the grain of the paper visible through the color.

6 The work on the leaves with very dense undiluted sap green gives the foliage mobility and creates a contrast with the sunlit fields.

7 Note how the contrast of the dark mass of the tree against the background of the panorama contributes to creating the elevated point of view we are concerned with in this exercise. It really feels as if we are looking down over the landscape from the top of one of the surrounding hills.

8 Now we begin the farm buildings by painting the roofs with a series of short diagonal damp strokes, alternating between pink, ochre, and yellow.

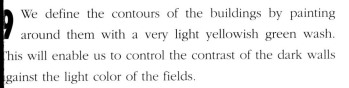

9 We define the contours of the buildings by painting around them with a very light yellowish green wash. This will enable us to control the contrast of the dark walls against the light color of the fields.

10 We are now painting the darker parts of the farmhouse with strokes of carmine mixed with burnt umber. These lines perfectly situate the plane of the roof in the walls of the building, and the windows appear to have depth.

11 The contrasts of the dark colors make the buildings appear three dimensional. Likewise, these contrasts contribute to making the farmhouse the composition's center of interest. We are creating a series of details (windows, adjoining roofs, and so on) relying on our observation of the subject rather than on the drawing.

DETAILS

Details are important when they are interesting. This is not just a play on words but a reality. A landscape contains attractive details that, for that very fact, should be incorporated into the picture. In a landscape, there is an infinite number of details, and it would be ridiculous to try to paint all of them. Instead, you should include only those that you like or the ones that most attract your attention.

12 The farmhouse has character. It is thanks to the windows and the shadows that we can make out the shapes of the walls and the different forms. The house appears to really stand on the terrain.

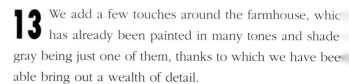

13 We add a few touches around the farmhouse, which has already been painted in many tones and shade gray being just one of them, thanks to which we have bee able bring out a wealth of detail.

14 The picture is finished. It was not difficult, but it was somewhat time-consuming. If you have followed these exercises, we are certain that you have grasped the techniques and art of watercolor.

ACKNOWLEDGMENTS

Very often, interesting but difficult
projects can be achieved only through
the collaboration of several people.
This book is an example of such a collaboration and has been possible thanks
to the following people:

Jordi Vigué, director of publications at Parramón Ediciones and a good friend, for his faith
and invaluable help and advice in writing this book;

Josep Guasch, for providing his knowledge and cre-
ative imagination in presenting the book in the clearest
and most attractive way;

Jordi Martínez, for his help in documenting the work and
resolving the thousand and one problems.

Finally, I wish to express my gratitude to Nos & Soto, for their magnificent
photography.

Vicenç Ballestar